Fascinating Facts about Fish

Thank you for purchasing this book.

You can find more books by this author by scanning the QR code below with your phone's camera (which will take you to the Author's Amazon page).

Table of Contents

Fish Species
Overview

Fish make up the largest group of vertebrates with an estimated 34,300 species worldwide.

Fifty eight percent of existing fish species live in saltwater, whilst forty one percent are freshwater fish. The remaining one percent are anadromous (fish such as the salmon) migrating up rivers from the sea to spawn.

Fish sizes vary greatly, from the world's smallest fish, the Schindleria brevipinguis, with a maximum size of 10mm; to the world's largest fish, the whale shark, at around forty feet long.

Categories of Fish

Fish can be categorised as bony, cartilaginous, or jawless.

Bony Fish
Bony fish are species that make up most of the living fish today and are identified by having a bony skeleton.

Cartilaginous Fish
Cartilaginous fish are a class distinguished by having a skeleton of cartilage rather than bone. These include sharks and rays.

Jawless Fish
Some examples of jawless fish include lamprey and hagfish. Lampreys are aquatic creatures with no jaws that resemble an eel. They have sucker mouths with horny teeth and a rasping tongue. Hagfish are a type of fish that lack jaws, fins, and stomachs. They have circular, sucker-like mouths.

Fish Evolution

Fish have evolved to thrive in almost every aquatic environment on Earth.

Fish have been around for approximately 530 million years and are believed to have evolved from animals that were similar to sea squirts, which developed into fish-like creatures.

During the Devonian Period (between approximately 419 million and 359 million years ago), fish evolution advanced dramatically. The Devonian Period is known as the "Age of Fishes" because of the abundance, diversity, and, in some cases, bizarre fish species that swam the Devonian seas. During this time, different kinds of fish evolved, including bony fish and cartilaginous fish.

Prehistoric Fish

Interesting facts about prehistoric fish:

Dunkleosteus was a prehistoric fish that existed approximately 360 million years ago and could reach a maximum length of 33 feet. Its jaw was so strong that it could generate a tremendous bite force. According to an analysis of the jawbones of Dunkleosteus, it could bite with a force of approximately 8,000 pounds per square inch, putting it in the same league as the much later Tyrannosaurus rex.

Figure 1 Group of Dunkleosteus

Arandaspis is one of the oldest known species of fish, having existed approximately 470 million years ago. It measured approximately 15 centimetres in length and lacked fins. It propelled itself with its flattened tail, as a modern tadpole would.

Coelacanths are ancient fish that have existed for more than 360 million years and were once believed to be extinct.

Megalodon, a prehistoric shark that existed approximately 23 million years ago, was the largest shark ever to have existed. It could reach a length of sixty feet.

Ancient Fish Art

The Australian rock shelter Nawarla Gabarnmang contains some of the earliest fish-themed cave paintings. They are estimated to be 28,000 years old.

Two caves in France and Spain contain paintings of prehistoric fish. The fish relief at the Abri du Poisson ("Fish Rock Shelter") in France dates to approximately 23,000 BCE.

In La Pasiega Cave in the Cantabria region of Spain, fish-themed cave paintings were discovered. The fish depictions, which include salmon, trout, and eels, are believed to be approximately 20,000 years old.

Figure 2 Ubirr Fish rock art

A drawing of a halibut discovered in the La Pileta Cave in Spain dates to approximately 18,000 BCE. Because these caves are in regions that historically supported large fish populations, it is likely that the paintings were created by individuals who were engaged in fishing.

The Lascaux Cave in France contains additional prehistoric fish paintings. Here, numerous Palaeolithic cave paintings depict a variety of fish and other animals. It is estimated that they are approximately 17,000 years old.

The Nile Perch held a significant place in ancient Egyptian art, and it is depicted in several artworks. The tomb of the 18th dynasty nobleman Menna contains a painting depicting a Nile Perch.

In Magna Graecia in the fourth century BCE, fish-themed serving platters were exceptionally popular (a collection of ancient Greek cities in southern Italy).

Figure 3 Mosaic in Arian Baptistry, Ravenna, Italy

In Roman mosaics, fish were frequently depicted in abundance. The Lod Mosaic, discovered in the Israeli city of Lod around 300 C.E., is a particularly intricate and beautiful example.

Fish Anatomy
Fins

Fins are complex structures with multiple functions in fish and other aquatic animals.

Fins can be paired or unpaired, and their shapes, sizes, and compositions can vary based on how certain species have adapted.

Fins help fish swim, steer, maintain balance, stop, and glide. Some species use them to walk, rest, cool down, stun prey, display, defend, lure prey, and attach to other organisms.

Types of Fins

Pectoral fins (paired) - located on the sides of the fish, behind the gills. These fins are used for manoeuvring, braking, and balancing.

Pelvic fins (paired) - located on the underside of the fish, near the head. These fins are used for balancing and braking.

Dorsal fin - located on the back of the fish. This fin helps the fish stay upright and stable.

Adipose fin - a small fin located between the dorsal fin and the caudal fin on some species of fish. Its function is not well understood.

Anal fin - located on the underside of the fish, near the tail. This fin helps with stability and steering.

Caudal (tail) fin - located at the end of the fish's body. This fin propels the fish forward.

Figure 4 Mirror Carp - illustrating fins

Pectoral Fins

Flying Fish: Some species of flying fish have large pectoral fins that they use for gliding.

Mudskippers have pectoral fins that are located beneath their elongated body. These fins are articulated and function similarly to limbs, allowing the amphibious mudskipper to crawl on land.

Frogfish have modified pectoral fins that resemble legs, allowing them to "walk" along the ocean floor in search of food.

Pelvic Fins

In certain species, such as gobies and blennies, the pelvic fins are fused to form a suction cup, allowing the fish to adhere to rocks and other surfaces.

Males of certain species of cichlids display their pelvic fins to attract a mate. Females are attracted to fins that are vividly coloured or have distinctive patterns.

In certain fish species, such as guppies and swordtails, the male pelvic fins are modified into a gonopodium, which is used to transfer sperm to the female during mating.

The male stickleback uses his pelvic fins to fan water over their eggs in order to provide oxygen and keep them clean.

Dorsal Fins

Most species have only one dorsal fin, but some have two or three.

The sailfish has the largest dorsal fin among all fish species. The dorsal fin of a sailfish can be as tall as 1.5 meters (5 feet) and as long as the body of the fish itself.

The anterior of the dorsal fin of anglerfish is modified to resemble a fishing rod and a lure, which they use to attract prey.

Some catfish can extend the leading ray of their dorsal fin to deter predators or wedge themselves into crevices.

During aggressive encounters, the dorsal fin of a male Siamese fighting fish, also known as a betta fish, can be used to intimidate and repel other males.

Adipose Fins

The adipose fin is absent in many fish families, but found in salmon, characids, and catfish.

The function of the adipose fin is somewhat unknown. Information released in 2011 suggested that the fin may be essential for detecting and responding to stimuli such as touch, sound, and pressure changes. In 2014, Canadian researchers discovered a neural network in the fin, suggesting that it has a likely sensory function.

Anal Fins

The anal fin is also known as the cloacal fin.

Gymnotiform locomotion is a type of propulsion that is characterised by the undulations of a long anal fin, as observed in South American Knifefish.

Ocean Sunfish use their large anal fin in combination with their dorsal fin for propulsion.

The Black Skirt Tetra derives its name from its flowing anal fin. The fin spans nearly half of the length of the fish.

Caudal (Tail) Fins

The caudal fin is the tail fin - from the Latin cauda meaning tail.

Thresher Shark uses its elongated tail to whip unsuspecting prey, which stuns the fish before it is consumed. The fastest strikes approach 50 mph.

Seahorses are the only type of fish with tails that can grab objects, called prehensile tails.

Stingrays have venomous spines on their tails normally used for defence.

Venomous Fins

Lionfish are well-known for their venomous fin spines, which can cause painful but rarely fatal puncture wounds.

Scorpionfish are members of the Scorpaenidae family, which contains the most poisonous fish. It has spines on its dorsal, pelvic, and anal fins.

Stonefish are also members of the Scorpaenidae family and

have spines on their dorsal, pelvic, and anal fins.

Weever fish have needle-sharp and poisonous spines along their backs. People are occasionally stung after stepping on weevers partially buried in the sand.

Swim Bladder

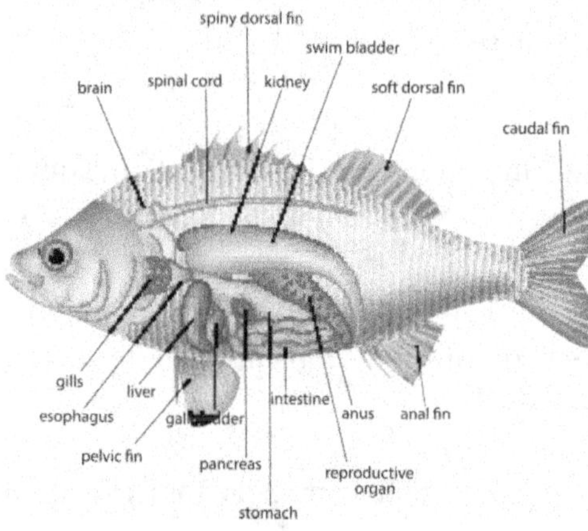

Figure 5 Fish anatomy

The swim bladder is an internal gas-filled organ that allows many bony fish to control their buoyancy and maintain their current water depth without expending energy in swimming.

In most fish, the swim bladder consists of two gas-filled sacs located in the fish's dorsal region. However, in a few primitive species, there is only one gas-filled sac. It has walls that contract or expand in response to the surrounding pressure.

The mixture of gases in the bladder is variable. The ratios of shallow water fish closely resemble those of the atmosphere, whereas deep sea fish tend to have higher oxygen concentrations.

Internal adjustments enable the fish to achieve neutral

buoyancy and ascend and descend to a wide range of depths. This position of the swim bladder also provides the fish with lateral stability.

Not every fish has a swim bladder. Some bottom-dwelling and deep-sea bony fish (teleosts) and all cartilaginous fish lack a swim bladder.

Cartilaginous fish as sharks and rays lack swim bladders. Some of them can only control their depth by swimming, while others store fats or oils with a lower density than seawater to produce a neutral or near-neutral buoyancy.

The interface between gas and tissue of the swim bladder produces a strong sound reflection, which is used by sonar equipment to locate fish.

During World War II, sonar operators using newly developed sonar technology were perplexed by what appeared to be a false sea floor 300–500 metres deep during the day and shallower at night. This was the result of millions of marine organisms, primarily small mesopelagic fish, whose swim bladders reflected the sonar.

The swim bladder can also radiate sound pressure, enhancing the animal's hearing and sensitivity.

Some species, primarily freshwater fishes such as common carp and catfish, have a connection between the swim bladder and the inner ear. They are connected by Weberian ossicles, which consist of four bones. These bones are capable of transmitting vibrations and are well-suited for detecting sound and vibrations. This improves the fish's hearing ability.

Fish Scales

The word 'scale' is derived from the Old French word 'escale,' which means a shell pod or husk.

Fish scales are small, rigid plates that grow out of a fish's skin. Scales' main function is to provide the fish with protection. They can also serve as camouflage due to their colouration and reflectivity.

Figure 6 Roach scales

Scales vary greatly in size, shape, structure, and coverage, ranging from robust and rigid armour plates in shrimpfishes and boxfishes to microscopic or non-existent in eels and catfish.

In bony fishes, the scales along the lateral line have central pores that allow water to contact the sensory cells.

The scales of porcupine fishes have evolved into large external spines.

Some herrings and anchovies have scales that are easily shed, allowing them to evade predators.

Aristotle (ca. 340 B.C.) may have been the first scientist to speculate on the use of hard parts of fishes to determine age, stating in 'Historica Animalium' that "the age of a scaly fish may be told by the size and hardness of its scales."

The age of fish can be determined by counting the number of annuli (rings) on a scale.

Some fish, including surgeonfish and butterflyfish, have scales with electromagnetic properties. It is believed that the electromagnetic properties of fish scales serve a variety of purposes, including:

Navigation: Fish scales can help fish to sense the Earth's magnetic field, enabling them to navigate in murky water or to find their way back to their home reefs.

Communication: Scales can also be used to communicate with other fish. By sending out electromagnetic waves, fish can communicate their location, size, and species.

Defence: Scales can also be used for protection against predators. By reflecting electromagnetic waves, fish can make themselves appear to predators as larger or more dangerous.

Some parrotfish species have scales that can withstand a spear.

In some cultures, fish scales are used for decorative purposes. In Native American cultures, fish scales were frequently used to create intricate patterns on clothing and accessories.

In the seventeenth century it was discovered that an extract from fish scales could be used to make imitation pearls. It was first used in France using the scales of the bleak.

'Pearl essence' is composed of guanine, an iridescent compound found in fish scales. Guanine in its crystalline form reflects and refracted light. The guanine suspension in a solvent is known as "essence of pearls." It is used in cosmetics to create a shimmering effect.

Fish Colours

The colours of fish are produced by pigments in their skin, scales, and eyes. The most common pigments are melanin, carotenoids, and pteridines.

Melanin is responsible for giving fish their dark colours, including black, brown, and grey. Additionally, it is used to shield fish from UV radiation.

Carotenoids are the pigments responsible for the red, orange, and yellow hues of fish. They are derived from the fish's diet and frequently serve as indicators of health and fertility.

Pteridines are responsible for giving fish their blue and green hues. Additionally, they are used to shield fish from UV radiation.

Fish have evolved a vast array of colours and patterns to help them blend into their environment and avoid predators. This is referred to as cryptic colouring.

Some fish use their vibrant colours and patterns to attract mates and ward off predators. This is known as aposematic coloration.

Several fish can change colour rapidly to adapt to their environment and disguise themselves. A particular type of iridophore in the scales of chameleon sand tilefish is activated by an adrenaline response, allowing the fish to change colour from blue-green to red in half a second.

Colour and colour pattern are the most important quality criteria dictating the market value of Koi carp. Good water quality and a diet containing both natural and artificial colour enhancers are used by breeders to achieve vibrant colouration.

Teeth

Depending on their diets, fish have evolved to have various types of teeth. Herbivorous fish may have broad, flat teeth used for grinding plant matter, while carnivorous fish may have pointed, sharp teeth used for killing and capturing prey.

Figure 7 Shark showing formidable teeth

Almost all species of fish have teeth, but sea horses and adult sturgeon do not.

Sharks continually replace their rows of teeth throughout their lives. When a tooth is lost, a new tooth emerges to take its place. Other fish, such as bony fish, have permanent, nonregenerative teeth.

Many sharks have teeth in layered rows. On average, sharks possess fifteen rows and five series of teeth, for a total of up to 300 teeth.

Depending on what they consume, sharks can lose several teeth per week. When a tooth is lost, a replacement tooth typically emerges to take its place. They can lose thousands of teeth throughout their lifetimes.

The largest fish tooth ever found belonged to a Megalodon. Megalodon was the largest fish ever known - a type of shark that could reach lengths of around 60 to 70 feet. Their teeth were up to 18cm long.

The fish with the largest teeth relative to its head size is the Sloan's viperfish (Chauliodus sloani), which must open its mouth to make the jaws vertical before it can swallow prey. When the mouth is shut, the teeth extend beyond the jaws.

The frontal teeth of the Sheepshead fish closely resembling human teeth, which enable them to crush the shells of prey.

Piranhas are notorious for their razor-sharp teeth and aggressive bite. In the Brazilian language Tupi, the word piranha means "tooth fish."

Figure 8 Pike showing its teeth

Pharyngeal Teeth

Pharyngeal teeth are teeth located in the pharyngeal arch of the throat of certain fish species that lack teeth elsewhere, such as cyprinids, suckers, and other fish species. These teeth are used to grind food and aid in digestion.

The pharyngeal jaws are a "second set" of jaws contained in an animal's throat, or pharynx, distinct from the oral jaws.

Certain species of fish, including Clown Loaches and Grunts, produce distinctive sounds when they grind their pharyngeal teeth.

The size and shape of pharyngeal teeth vary due to dietary differences. Large, pointed pharyngeal teeth enable certain species of marine fish to shred shrimp, fish, and other soft prey. Large, flat pharyngeal teeth are adapted to transmit the heavy forces necessary to crush tough prey.

Swimming and Leaping
Swimming

Fastest Swimmers
10 fastest fish in the world:

1. Sailfish - 68 mph (110 km/h)

2. Swordfish - 60 mph (97 km/h)

3. Marlin - 50 mph (80 km/h)

4. Wahoo - 48 mph (77 km/h)

5. Yellowfin Tuna - 46 mph (74 km/h)

6. Bluefin Tuna - 43 mph (69 km/h)

7. Mako Shark - 43 mph (69 km/h)

8. Bonefish - 40 mph (64 km/h)

9. Rainbow Runner - 40 mph (64 km/h)

10. Barracuda - 36 mph (58 km/h)

Stamina
The common carp can swim for long periods without getting tired, covering up to 124 miles (200 kilometres) in a single journey.

Slowest Swimmers
The slowest fish is the sea anemone fish, also known as the clownfish, which has a maximum swimming speed of just 5 miles per hour (8 kilometres per hour).

Leaping

Why Fish Leap

Here are some reasons why fish leap out of the water:

To avoid predators.

To overcome obstacles when migrating.

When startled.

To capture prey.

To get rid of external parasites.

Mating display.

Take in oxygen.

Leap between bodies of water.

Figure 9 Mobula ray jumping out of water

Fish Leaping Statistics

Some Asian carp species have been observed to leap as high as 10 feet (3 metres) from the water. This behaviour can be dangerous for boaters, as fish can collide with vessels and cause damage and injury.

The Silver Carp is another species of carp recognised for its ability to leap. When they hear loud noises or sense water vibrations, they are known to leap up to 8 feet (2.4 metres) out of the water.

During their annual migration to spawn, trout can leap up to

3-6 feet (1-2 metres) out of the water, depending on the species.

Salmon must traverse waterfalls and other obstacles during their annual migration to spawn in order to reach spawning grounds. Salmon can leap as high as 1 to 3 feet (0.3 to 0.3 m), depending on the species and certain species of migrating Trout can leap 3 to 6 feet (1 to 2 m) overcoming similar obstacles.

Figure 10 Atlantic Salmon leaping

The Indo-Pacific sailfish is one of the highest jumping fish, having been observed to leap as high as 10 feet (3 metres) out of the water. Great White Sharks can lunge up to 8 to 10 feet (2.4 to 3.3 metres) out of the water, especially when breaching to capture prey.

In May 2008, a film crew in Japan captured on camera a flying fish that flew for 45 seconds, establishing a new record.

Fish Senses
Taste and Smell

Fish have an advanced sense of taste and smell, which they use for various purposes such as finding food, avoiding predators, and navigating their environment.

Fish have a highly developed olfactory system, which is their ability to smell. One or two pairs of nostrils (nares) allow water to enter the nasal cavity of fish. Inside the nasal cavity is the olfactory epithelium, which contains the sensory cells that detect molecules dissolved in water and are responsible for detecting odours in the water. Fish can detect a wide variety of dissolved chemical substances, including pheromones released by other fish.

Fish have diversely developed olfactory organs. At one extreme, they are well developed, as in sharks and eels, while at the other extreme, they are poorly developed, as in pike and sticklebacks.

Chemoreceptors are specialised cells that are present in the nostrils, mouth, and skin of fish. These receptors can detect and react to chemical cues in the water, allowing fish to detect predators, find potential mates, and locate food sources. They can detect even minute chemical changes in water.

Fish have taste buds all over their bodies, including on their fins, in their mouths, and even on their skin. These taste buds enable them to detect chemicals in water and determine the flavour of food they consume. Fish can distinguish between tastes such as sweet, sour, salty, and bitter.

When returning to spawn from the ocean, salmon use olfactory cues to identify their home stream.

When young fish begin migrating to the ocean, they begin to build their "smell memory bank." This is referred to as olfactory imprinting.

Catfish have a highly developed sense of smell and taste and can detect specific substances at extremely low concentrations, enabling them to locate food from a distance. Catfish possess over 250,000 taste buds. The mouth and gill rakers are densely populated with taste buds, and the catfish's sensory organs extend to the whiskers, fins, back, belly, sides, and even the tail.

Sharks have an acute sense of smell that enables them to detect certain substances at exceptionally low concentrations. Sharks can smell blood from hundreds of meters away in concentrations as low as one part per million (ppm).

Barbules or Whiskers

Barbules are thin, whisker-like sensory organs found near the mouth of some fish species. Catfish, carp, goatfish, hagfish, sturgeon, zebrafish, black dragonfish, and certain species of shark such as the sawshark have barbules.

Barbules, which contain these fish's taste buds, are used to locate food in murky water, silt, or gravel.

The origin of the word barbule is

Figure 11 Catfish - barbules

Middle Latin for barbula, which means "small beard."

Barbules can appear as small, fleshy projections or as long, cylindrical extensions of a fish's head and the barbules' muscle tissue allows for limited movement.

Taste buds are concentrated on the barbule. Concentrations of taste buds vary from species to species. Some catfish have twenty-five taste buds in a square millimetre of barbule skin.

Hearing

Because the speed of sound in water is approximately four times faster than in air, sound travels more efficiently and over greater distances underwater.

Fish rely on their hearing to locate prey, avoid predators, and communicate with their own kind.

Fish can detect sound through their lateral lines and otoliths (inner ears).

Hearing is well-developed in carp, which have the Weberian organ, a specialized structure that transfers vibrations in the swim bladder to the inner ear.

Although fish can hear, their hearing is limited to low frequencies. A small number of fish can hear frequencies between 3,000 and 4,000 Hz, whereas most fish can only hear between 800 and 1,000 Hz. Research showed that the American shad (Alosa sapidissima), can detect sounds up to 180,000 Hz (The human frequency range is typically cited as 20 to 20,000 Hz'.)

Lateral Line

The lateral lines of a fish's body are typically visible as faint pores running lengthwise along each side.

The lateral line is a system of tactile sense organs made up of receptors called neuromasts, clusters of hair-like cells, arranged in rows or canals along the head and body.

The lateral line system detects movement, vibration, and pressure gradients in the water surrounding an animal, providing spatial awareness and the capacity to navigate the environment. This is crucial for orientation, predator avoidance, and schooling.

Modified neuromasts known as electroreceptors are present in some species such as sharks and rays. These organs can detect electric fields produced by living organisms and the magnetic field of the Earth. These electroreceptors are concentrated on the heads of these fishes and are called Ampullae of Lorenzini.

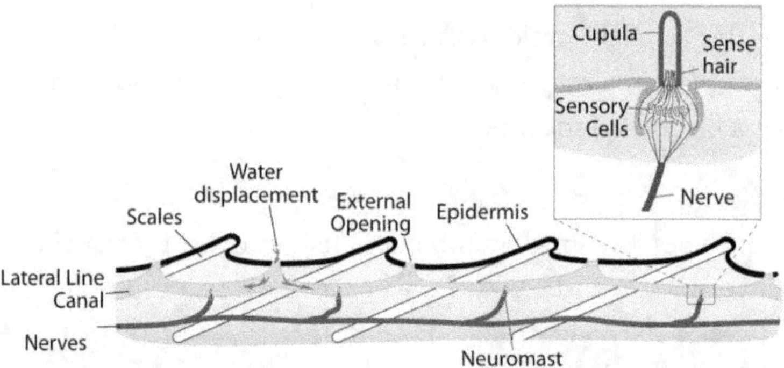

Figure 12 Lateral line organ

Communication by Sound

Fish use grunts, pops, chirps, and other sounds to communicate with each other. These sounds are generated in various ways:

Swim Bladder
Some fish make noise with their swim bladders.

Male oyster toadfish use their swim bladders to make drumming sounds to attract females. The fast-twitch swim bladder muscles of toadfish can contract as much as 300 times per second.

Plainfin midshipman fish are found off the west coast of North America. In California, they are sometimes called "California singing fish." Throughout the mating season, the male hums by striking his swim bladder with his sonic muscle, sometimes for extended periods. His humming is intended to entice females.

Hydrodynamics
Using the water itself, fish can also generate sounds underwater. When spawning, parrotfish move rapidly back and forth through the water, creating a turbulent sound.

Stridulation
Stridulatory sounds are produced when hard skeletal parts or teeth are rubbed or hit together.

Seahorses produce clicking sounds by rubbing two parts of their skull together.

Marine catfishes have specialised pectoral fin spines that make a squeaking sound. Sound is created when the pectoral fin is rubbed against the pectoral girdle.

Loudest

According to new research, Gulf corvina are the noisiest fish in the world. Marine biologists who recorded the sound describe the creatures as "the loudest fish ever recorded."

Their microphones recorded individual calls that reached 177 decibels, about as loud as a lawn mower.

Sight

Though comparable to the eyes of birds and mammals, fish's eyes have a more spherical lens but can be slightly elliptical in some species. Birds and mammals adjust focus by altering the lens's shape, whereas fish adjust focus by moving the lens closer to or farther from the retina.

Figure 13 Baltic Herring — eyes

A fish's cornea is very rounded, allowing a wide field of view, of up to 360°. A human's field of view is around 180°.

Most species can perceive colour. Some fish can see ultraviolet light, and some are sensitive to polarised light.

Because water absorbs light, the amount of available light decreases with increasing depth. The shorter wavelengths like red, orange, and yellow disappear first and appear as shades of grey. The longer wavelengths of green and blue can penetrate further underwater before being absorbed.

Different wavelengths of light are absorbed to varying degrees. Ultraviolet light can penetrate deeper than visible light.

Fish living in shallow, clear water typically have better all-round colour vision. Deep-sea fish such as whiting and conger eels have large eyes with more rods, allowing them to detect more light in environments that are typically dark.

Eye Movement

Some species of fish can move their eyes independently such as the Sand lance and Pipefish can move their eyes independently. Flounders, too, have eyes on top of their heads and can move them independently to widen their field of vision.

Strange Eyes

Some species of fish have very strange-looking eyes:

Barreleyes have large, telescopic eyes that protrude from the skull. Their eyes are directed upwards, but some species possess the ability to swivel them forwards.

The European plaice is a flatfish with raised eyes, so it can still see when it buries itself in the sand for camouflage.

As a flatfish matures, the bones in its skull begin to twist and move. One eye begins to migrate from one side of the head to the other, resulting in two eyes on the same side.

Two species of tropical American river fishes of the genus Anableps are four-eyed fishes. They are surface dwellers and have eyes adapted for seeing both above and below the water surface.

Large Eyes

Larger specimens of the aptly named bigeye thresher shark (Alopias superciliosus) have eyeballs that can span more than 10 cm (3.9 in) and up to 12.5 cm (4.9 in).

Blind Cave Fish

The Mexican tetra (Astyanax mexicanus), also known as the blind cave fish, blind cave characin, and blind cave tetra. Cave-dwelling forms can have degenerated sight or have total loss of sight. The fish in the Pachón caves have completely lost their eyes, whereas the fish in the Micos cave have only limited vision.

Figure 14 Astyanax fasciatus mexicanus - Blind Cave Fish

Feeding
Diet

Based on their diet, fish can be either an herbivore, a carnivore, or an omnivore. Most fish are omnivores and consume both plant and animal matter for nutrition.

Some species, including tilapia, are primarily herbivorous and feed on phytoplankton and other plants.

Several species are hypercarnivorous (an animal which has a diet that is more than 70% meat, either by active predation or by scavenging). Examples of hypercarnivorous fish include sharks, barracuda, pike/muskellunge, walleye, and perch.

Cannibalism

Numerous fish species are cannibalistic and will consume their own kind if given the opportunity.

Fish can become cannibalistic as a result of stress induced by various environmental and population factors. It can also serve as a protective measure against a population's excessive density and as an alternative food source when other food resources become scarce.

Numerous fish species engage in filial cannibalism, in which a parent eats its own offspring. Many species of fish with paternal care will engage in total or partial clutch cannibalism in order to gain additional energy and nutrients, which may ultimately improve their reproductive success in the future.

Scale-Eating

Some fish consume the scales of other species. This is referred to as Lepidophagy. Numerous fish species have adapted specialised teeth and mouth structures that allow them to feed more efficiently on the scales of other fish.

Specialised Feeding

Some fish have specialised feeding habits, such as the mudskipper, which uses its fins to travel on land and eat insects and other small animals.

Figure 15 Mudskipper

The long snouts of certain predatory fish and the sucker mouths of bottom-dwelling fish are examples of specialised adaptations that aid in efficient feeding.

Some fish have a distinctive feeding behaviour known as "ram feeding," in which they swim rapidly through the water with their mouths wide open in order to capture prey. Whale sharks and Tuna use this method of feeding.

Lampreys are eel-like fish and use a specialised method of feeding in which they use their teeth to bore holes into the body of their prey and then insert their barb-covered tongue.

Temperature Extremes

Coldwater Species

Some species of cold-water fish can survive in water temperatures that are close to freezing.

To survive in cold water environments, these fish have evolved various adaptations, such as special proteins in their blood, which prevent ice crystals from forming in their tissues, and a slower metabolic rate, which allows them to conserve energy in food-scarce environments.

Here are a few examples:

Lake Whitefish (Coregonus clupeaformis) is found in cold water habitats throughout North America and can tolerate water temperatures as low as 33°F (0.6 °C).

Arctic Grayling (Thymallus arcticus) lives in cold water habitats throughout the northern hemisphere's circumpolar regions, including the Arctic, and can survive in water temperatures as low as 32°F (0°C).

The Arctic Char (Salvelinus alpinus) inhabits cold water habitats throughout the northern hemisphere, including the Arctic, and can survive in water temperatures as low as 32°F (0°C).

Warmwater Species

Warm-water fish inhabit regions where the water temperature exceeds 80°F (27°C), such as the tropics and subtropics Here are some examples:

Largemouth Bass: Largemouth bass can tolerate water temperatures up to 90°F (32 °C) and can be found in lakes, rivers, and reservoirs across North America.

Catfish can tolerate water temperatures up to 95°F (35°C) and can be found in rivers and lakes all over the world.

Snakehead fish are indigenous to Asia and Africa and can withstand water temperatures as high as 96°F (35°C).

The Julimes pupfish (Cyprinodon julimes) is endemic to El Pandeño, a hot spring in Julimes, Chihuahua, Mexico, and has adapted to life in water that reaches temperatures as high as 46 °C (114 °F).

Figure 16 Julimes pupfish

The bighead pupfish (Cyprinodon pachycephalus) is a critically endangered species of pupfish endemic to an area covering less than 1 km2 (0.4 sq. mi) at San Diego de Alcala in the Conchos River basin, Chihuahua of Mexico. It inhabits hot springs, their outflows, and an impoundment pool containing water as hot as 49 °C (120 °F).

Reproduction and Eggs
Reproduction

Most fish species rely on external fertilisation – a fusion of sperm and eggs. During spawning, members of a species group together and release their eggs and sperm simultaneously. This enhances fertilisation and improves the survival rate of eggs, even in the presence of predators. Young fish are left without parental protection.

Some species protect their young in various ways:

A few fish species release their eggs but keep them nearby, sometimes forming a nest, and guard them until they hatch. Siamese fighting fish males build bubble nests and protect the eggs until they hatch.

Male seahorses carry the fertilized eggs in a special pouch on their stomachs until they hatch.

Some species collect fertilised eggs in their mouths and protect them until they hatch, a process known as mouthbrooding. These include: Apogonidae (cardinalfish), Ariidae (sea catfish), and numerous species of Cichlidae (cichlids).

The male three-spined stickleback constructs a nest of vegetation in which the female lays up to 400 eggs. The male then defends the nest from other fish until the young hatch, which can take up to four weeks.

Figure 17 Stickleback

Several fish species can change their sex. These fish are known as sequential hermaphrodites because they first develop into males before maturing into females. Clownfish, Asian Sheepshead Wrasse, and Mangrove Rivulus are a few examples.

Oviparity
Oviparity: Most fish species undergo external fertilization and for most fish species, the eggs develop outside of the mother's body. This form of development is known as oviparity.

Ovoviviparity
Ovoviviparity: Most shark and ray species develop their eggs inside their bodies without receiving direct nourishment from the mother. Embryos are nourished internally from a yolk sac a process known as ovoviviparity. Eggs hatch inside the mother's body and young are delivered alive. Fish that give birth to live young are called livebearers.

Viviparity

Viviparity: Egg development is different in viviparous fish, and the embryo is directly attached to and nourished by the mother's body.

Parthenogenesis

Some fish species can reproduce without a mate, a process called parthenogenesis.

Parthenogenesis is an asexual reproduction process in which an egg develops into an embryo without the use of sperm. The blacktip shark, bonnethead shark, and zebra shark are examples of fish species that reproduce through parthenogenesis.

Bizarre Reproductive Behaviour

Anglerfish have a unique reproductive strategy known as sexual parasitism.

Males use their jaws to attach to females, and in some cases, the tissues and circulatory systems of both sexes are joined. The transformation renders him completely dependent on her and the male simply acts as a sperm-producing organ for her.

Fish Egg Facts

Eggs are typically round but can also be ellipsoidal and even pear-shaped.

The colour of fish eggs can range from translucent to opaque, such as gold or neon.

Fish eggs can take anywhere from a few days to several months to hatch, depending on the species and conditions.

Many other aquatic animals, including birds, amphibians, and other fish, rely on fish eggs as a food source.

Changes in water temperature, pH levels, and other environmental factors are extremely sensitive to fish eggs. Even minor changes in these conditions can have a significant impact on egg survival and the fish that hatch from them.

Fish Egg Statistics
The tiniest eggs can be as small as a pin's head, measuring around 0.04 inch (1 mm) in diameter for some species.

Female fish can lay from hundreds to several million eggs at a time, depending on the species.

Sunfish – (Mola mola) - up to 300 million eggs per female, each measuring 1.8 mm in diameter.

Ocean sunfish – (Mola alexandrini) - up to 300 million eggs per female, each measuring 1.8 mm in diameter.

Southern bluefin tuna – (Thunnus maccoyii) - up to 30 million eggs per female, each measuring 1.5 mm in diameter.

Pacific bluefin tuna – (Thunnus orientalis) - up to 10 million eggs per female, each measuring 1.2 mm in diameter.

Atlantic bluefin tuna – (Thunnus thynnus) - up to 10 million eggs per female, each measuring 1.2 mm in diameter.

Giant catfish – (Pangasianodon gigas) - up to 1 million eggs per female, each measuring 3.5 mm in diameter.

Sturgeon – (Acipenseridae family) - up to 1.5 million eggs per female, each measuring 3-4 mm in diameter.

Goliath grouper – (Epinephelus itajara) - up to 5 million eggs per female, each measuring 1 mm in diameter.

Lake sturgeon – (Acipenser fulvescens) - up to 200,000 eggs per female, each measuring 4 mm in diameter.

Atlantic salmon – (Salmo salar) - up to 4,000 eggs per female, each measuring 9 mm in diameter.

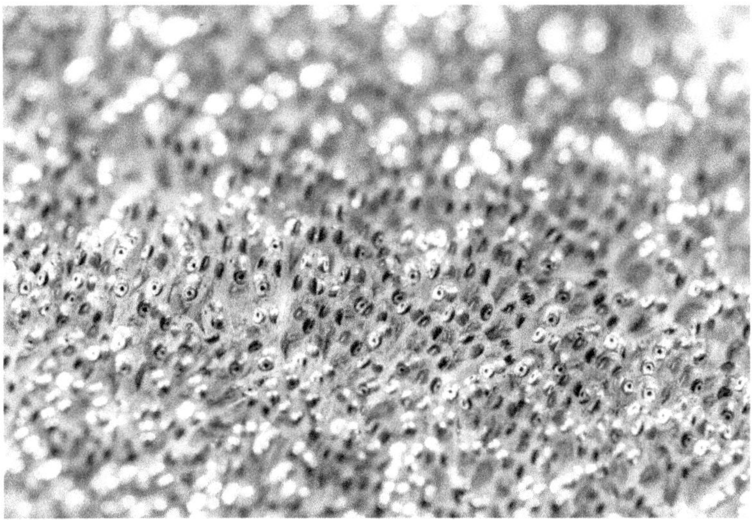

Figure 18 Clownfish eggs hours before hatching.

Fish Migration

The mass movement of fish from one area or body of water to another is known as fish migration. Many fish migrate on a regular basis, from daily to annually or more, and over distances ranging from a few metres to thousands of kilometres.

Migrations are frequently scheduled to coincide with food availability or to facilitate reproduction.

Scientists believe that fish use a variety of signals to navigate during migration, including the Earth's magnetic field, visual landmarks, and their sense of smell.

Migration Classifications

Migratory fishes are classified into three types: Oceanodromous, anadromous, and catadromous. Oceanodromous fish are those that live and migrate entirely in the sea. Anadromous fish migrate from the sea to fresh water to spawn. Catadromous fish migrate from fresh water to salt water to spawn.

Fish Species Migrations

Salmon are famous for their long journeys to spawning grounds. Some Pacific salmon species swim over a thousand miles upstream to spawn, frequently leaping over cascades and rapids.

Many eel species migrate to the ocean to spawn from freshwater rivers and streams. The European eel migrates up to 4,000 miles from European rivers to the Sargasso Sea in the Atlantic Ocean to spawn.

One of the most well-known fish migrations is that of the Atlantic bluefin tuna, which migrates from its spawning grounds in the Gulf of Mexico to its feeding grounds in the Mediterranean Sea and North Atlantic. The Pacific bluefin tuna also travels up to 6,000 miles across the ocean in a single year.

From May to July, billions of sardines, specifically the Southern African pilchard (Sardinops sagax), spawn in the cool waters of the Agulhas Bank and migrate north along the east coast of South Africa. Their vast numbers cause a coastal feeding frenzy. The run, which involves millions of sardines, happens when a cold water circulation from the Agulhas Bank flows north to Mozambique and then east into the Indian Ocean.

Figure 19 Bluefin tuna

The shortfin and longfin mako sharks migrate up to 6,000 miles per year.

Cod are found in the Atlantic Ocean and can migrate up to 1,000 miles between their feeding grounds and spawning grounds.

Deep-sea Migration

Some fish species migrate vertically, moving up and down the water column in response to shifting environmental conditions. This is especially common among deep-sea fish, which migrate to shallower depths at night to forage and return to deeper waters by day to avoid predators, this is known as Diel vertical migration (DVM). Fish such as Pacific sand lance, Striped bass and Bull sharks exhibit this behaviour.

Migration Adaptations

The Arctic char can adapt to changing environmental conditions by changing their migration patterns in response to changes in temperature or water level.

Euryhaline Organisms

These organisms can adapt to a wide range of salinities. An example of a euryhaline fish is the molly (Poecilia sphenops) which can live in fresh water, brackish water, or salt water. Other euryhaline fish species include the Atlantic stingray, bull shark, green chromide, and mummichog.

Stenohaline organisms, which can only survive in a narrow range of salinities, are the opposite of euryhaline organisms. Most freshwater organisms are stenohaline, meaning they will die in seawater, and most marine organisms are stenohaline, meaning they cannot live in fresh water.

Festivals and Cultural Traditions

Fish migration is celebrated with festivals and cultural traditions in some parts of the world. For example, the Haida people of Canada hold an annual salmon ceremony to honour the fish that sustains their culture.

World Fish Migration Day (WFMD)

WFMD is a one-day event, celebrated every other year, to create worldwide awareness of the importance of freshwater migratory fish and open rivers for the general public, especially students and their teachers, resource managers and engineers.

Figure 20 Schooling fish

Fish Superpowers

Electric abilities: Electric eels and electric rays can shock prey and repel predators by producing electric fields as strong as 600 volts.

Figure 21 Electric eel

Zebrafish are capable of regenerating body sections following injury.

Stonefish can blend in with their environment, rendering them virtually invisible and allowing them to ambush prey or hide from predators.

Deep-sea fish, such as the Lanternfish and Anglerfish, produce light through bioluminescence for communication, attracting prey, and distracting predators.

Anti-freeze Blood: The anti-freeze proteins in the blood of

cold-water inhabitants such as Arctic Cod and Antarctic Icefish prevent their cells from freezing.

Salmon and eels are equipped with a magnetic sense that helps them navigate during migration.

Deep-sea fish have adapted to extreme pressure and are able to survive at depths exceeding 8,000 metres.

Sailfish can swim at speeds of up to 68 miles per hour, ranking them the fastest fish in the ocean.

Poisonous Defence: Pufferfish produce substances that are lethal to their predators.

Chameleon fish are capable of changing their colour and pattern to blend in with their surroundings or communicate with other fish.

Walking catfish and Lungfish can breathe air in addition to water, allowing them to survive in environments with low oxygen levels.

Figure 22 Walking catfish

Symbiotic Relationships

Cleaner shrimp: These crustaceans remove parasites and dead skin cells from the scales of fish.

Cleaner Wrasse: Like Cleaner shrimp, Cleaner Wrasse eliminate parasites and dead skin from fish.

Remora: They have a suction cup on the tip of their heads, allowing them to attach to larger fish while feeding on leftovers from the larger fish's food.

Figure 23 Remora on shark's belly

Pilot fish: these small fish follow larger marine creatures such as sharks and feed on their leftovers.

Anglerfish, have bioluminescent bacteria that reside on their bodies and use their light to attract prey.

Goby: Some species of gobies have a symbiotic relationship with shrimp or crabs, in which the goby provides protection by keeping an eye out for predators while the shrimp or crab digs a burrow for the pair to reside in.

Anemonefish (also known as clownfish) inhabit the stinging tentacles of marine anemones, which protect them from predators while they feed the anemone.

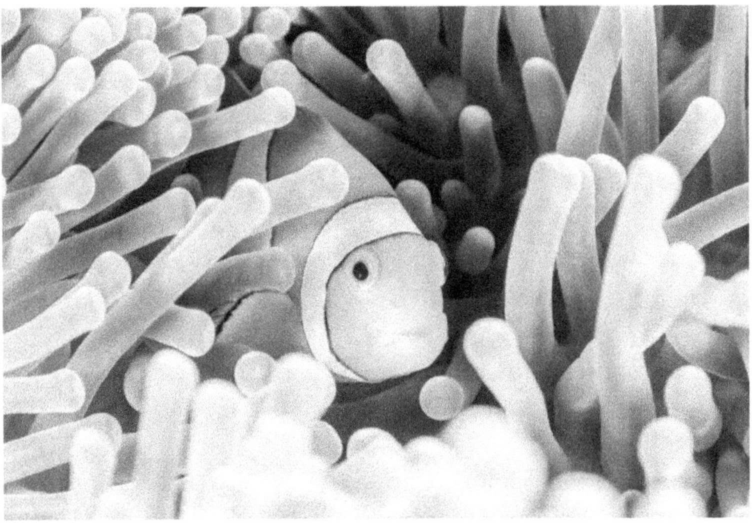

Figure 24 Clownfish

Some species of fish, such as tonguefish, have parasitic isopods that reside in their mouth, consume the fish's tongue, and then serve as a functional substitute for the tongue.

Records and Statistics
Biggest Game Fish Species

Figure 25 Game fishing rods.

Here are some of the biggest game fish caught on rod and line (International Game Fish Association listings 2023):

Marlin (Black) - 1560lbs - Cabo Blanco, Peru - 1953

Tuna (Bluefin) - 1496lbs - Nova Scotia, Canada - 1979

Marlin (Blue) -1402lbs - Vitoria, Brazil - 1992

Marlin (Striped) - 494lbs - Tutukaka, New Zealand - 1986

Halibut (Pacific) - 459lbs - Dutch Harbour, Alaska - 1996

Arapaima - 339lbs - Amazonia, Ecuador - 2010

Gar (Alligator) - 279lbs - Rio Grande, Texas - 1951

Tarpon - 286lbs - Rubane, Guinea-Bissau - 2003

Wahoo - 184lbs - Cabo San Lucas, Mexico - 2005

Amberjack - 163lbs - Zenisu, Japan - 2015

Giant Trevally - 160lbs - Kagoshima, Japan - 2006

Catfish (Blue) - 143lbs - Buggs Island, Virginia - 2011

Cobia - 135lbs - Shark Bay, Western Australia - 1985

Taimen - 115lbs - Tugur River, Russia - 2021

Rooster Fish - 114lbs - Baja California, Mexico - 1960

Barracuda (Guinean) - 102lbs - Barra du Kwanza, Angola - 2013

Salmon (Chinook) - 97lbs - Kenai River, Alaska - 1985

Salmon (Atlantic) - 79lbs - Tana River, Norway - 1928

Trout (Lake) - 72lbs - Great Bear Lake, Canada - 1995

Muskellunge - 67lbs - Lake Court Oreilles, Wisconsin - 1949

Permit - 60lbs - Ilha do Mel, Brazil - 2002

Snook (Pacific Black) - 59lbs - Quepos, Costa Rica - 2014

Dorado - 55lbs - Uruguay River, Argentina - 2006

Northern Pike - 55lbs - Lake of Greefern, Germany - 1986

Trout (Rainbow) - 48lbs - Lake Diefenbaker, Canada - 2009

Trout (Brown) - 44lbs - Ohau Canal, Twizel - NZ – 2020

Smallest Fish Species

Schindleria brevipinguis - The males of this species grow to be just 7.7 mm (0.3 inches) long, making them the smallest fish and one of the smallest vertebrates in the world. They are found in the waters around Australia and New Zealand.

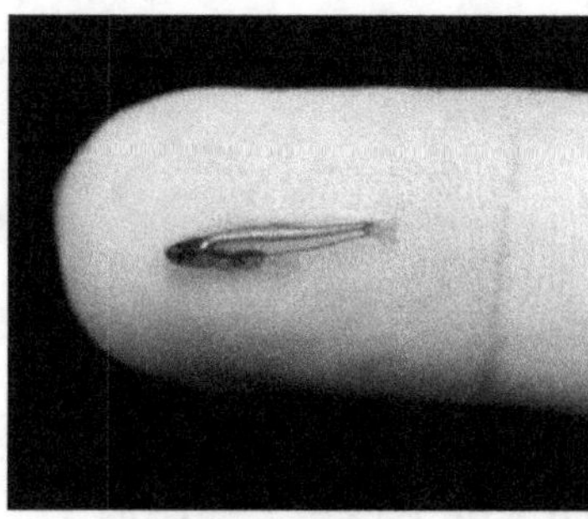

Figure 26 Schindleria brevipinguis

Paedocypris - Adult females of this species grow to be only 7.9 mm (0.3 inches) in length, This makes them one of the world's tiniest fish. They are found in swamps and streams on the Indonesian island of Sumatra.

Trimmatom nanus - This fish, which is native to Indonesia, grows to be only about 8 mm (0.3 inches) in length.

Paedocypris fisheloni - Another species in the Paedocypris genus, this fish grows to be just 8.4 mm (0.3 inches) long. It is found in the peat swamps of Indonesia.

Paedocypris micromegethes - This species is one of the smallest known vertebrates in the world, with females growing to be only 8.8 mm (0.35 inches) long. It is found in Indonesia.

Photocorynus spiniceps - This deep-sea fish, which is found in the waters around Hawaii, grows to be only about 9.7 mm (0.38 inches) in length.

Deep Sea Fish Species

Melanocetus johnsonii (deep-sea anglerfish) - depth range: 3,281-6,562 ft (1,000-2,000 m)

Chiasmodon niger (swallower) - depth range: 4,921-9,842 ft (1,500-3,000 m)

5. Pachystomias microdon - depth range: 4,921-9,842 ft (1,500-3,000 m)

Abyssocottus gibsoni (deep-sea sculpin) - depth range: 8,202-9,842 ft (2,500-3,000 m)

Xenodermichthys copei - depth range: 13,123-16,404 ft (4,000-5,000 m)

Bathymicrops regis (king of the abyss) - depth range: 16,404-19,685 ft (5,000-6,000 m)

Notacanthus chemnitzii - depth range: 16,404-19,685 ft (5,000-6,000 m)

Argyropelecus gigas - depth range: 3,281-16,404 ft (1,000-5,000 m)

Polyacanthonotus challengeri - depth range: 13,123-16,404 ft (4,000-5,000 m)

Paraliparis bathybius (deep-sea snailfish) - depth range: 13,123-19,685 ft (4,000-6,000 m)

Abyssocaris abyssorum - depth range: 16,404-19,685 ft (5,000-6,000 m)

Thalassobathia pelagica (deep-sea tadpolefish) - depth range:

16,404-19,685 ft (5,000-6,000 m)

On 15 August 2022, a juvenile Pseudoliparis snailfish (unknown species) was filmed investigating a baited camera 8,336 metres (27,499 feet) below the surface in the Izu-Ogasawara Trench in Japan. It is undisputedly the deepest fish in the world.

In one of the deepest parts of the ocean, the Mariana snailfish (Pseudoliparis swirei) has been discovered at depths of up to 8,178 metres (26,831 feet) in the Mariana Trench. This fish has adapted to extreme pressure, cold temperatures, and darkness, by having a high proportion of water in its body to counteract pressure and a gelatinous layer on its skin to protect itself from abrasion.

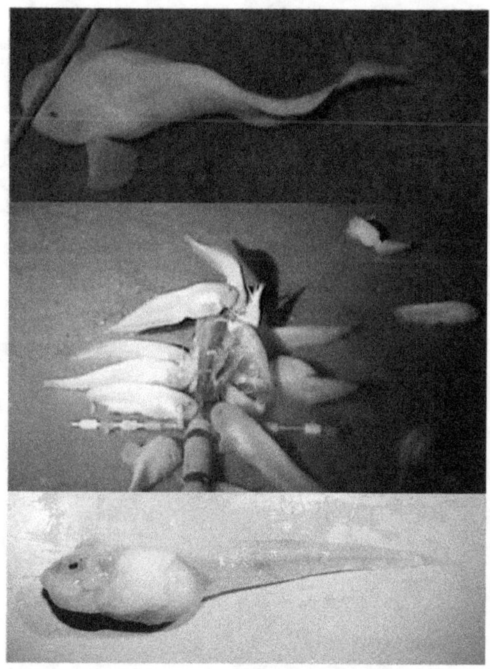

Figure 27 Pseudoliparis swirei

World's Ugliest Fish

Contenders for world's ugliest fish:

Blobfish: The Blobfish, which is commonly referred to as the "ugliest fish in the world," lives in the deep sea off the coasts of Australia and New Zealand. It resembles a blob due to its sagging, gelatinous appearance.

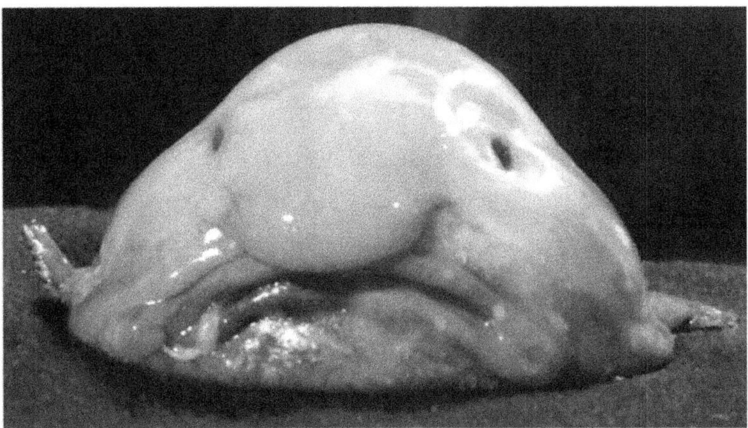

Figure 28 Blobfish

Fangtooth fish: The fangtooth fish has longer, sharper teeth in proportion to its body than any other fish species. It inhabits deep waters and has a small, scaled body that is disproportionate to its large head.

The Humpback Anglerfish: This fish has a large, bulbous body and a fleshy growth hanging in front of its mouth. It is also well-known for the bioluminescent lure on its head, which it uses to attract prey in the ocean's dark depths.

Stargazer: The stargazer is a fish with a large head, small eyes, and a wide, upward-facing mouth, which gives it the appearance of staring at the heavens. It has venomous spines on its back that it can use to defend itself.

The Goblin Shark is a deep-sea shark with an elongated snout and extendable jaws for capturing prey. Its pinkish-grey skin and peculiar features have earned it the name "living fossil."

The Frilled Shark has a body that resembles an eel and six pairs of gill slits, giving it a "frilly" appearance. It is a deep-sea predator with needle-like teeth that humans rarely encounter.

Coffinfish: A small fish with a coffin-shaped body and a hinged lower jaw, the Coffinfish. It resides in deep waters off the coasts of Australia and New Zealand and is sometimes referred to as the "sea toad" due to its bumpy texture.

The Sarcastic Fringehead is a small fish with a gaping mouth and tentacles that surround its head. It is infamous for its aggressive nature and fierce territorial defence against other fish.

Wolf fish: The wolf fish has a long, slimy body and sharp fangs, which it uses to crush its prey's shells. It is frequently described as having a prehistoric or extra-terrestrial appearance.

Sloan's viperfish: Its primary characteristic is its enormous teeth. When the jaw is closed, the teeth form a cage that is likely capable of trapping prey. It can open its mouth up to 90 degrees, allowing it to catch prey up to 63 percent of its own body size.

Longest Fish in the World

1. Whale Shark - 41.5 feet (12.65 meters)

2. Giant Oarfish - up to 36 feet (11 meters)

3. Basking Shark - 32.8 feet (10 meters)

4. Greenland Shark - up to 24 feet (7.3 meters)

5. Chinese Paddlefish - up to 23 feet (7 meters)

6. Great White Shark - 20.3 feet (6.2 meters)

7. Beluga Sturgeon - up to 20 feet (6 meters)

8. Alligator Gar - up to 10 feet (3 meters)

9. Arapaima - up to 10 feet (3 meters)

10. Mekong Giant Catfish - up to 9.8 feet (3 meters)

Figure 29 Whale shark

Most Expensive Fish
Koi

Koi are a variety of ornamental carp cultivated for their distinctive colours and patterns. The crimson and white Kohaku variety is highly prized for its beauty and symmetry. Taisho Sanke, Showa Sanshoku, and Yamabuki Ogon are also highly prized Koi varieties.

The world's priciest fish is the Japanese Koi, particularly the Kohaku variety. These fish have become a symbol of wealth and prestige in Japan, where they can be sold for millions of dollars.

The most expensive Koi ever sold was 'S Legend,' a Kohaku winner of the All-Japan Koi Show. This 9-year-old Koi masterpiece was sold for a staggering £1.4M/203 million Yen during a furious bidding war.

Figure 30 Koi

Most Expensive Aquarium Fish

Here are some of the world's most expensive aquarium fish:

The most expensive aquarium fish that has been sold on record was a Flowerhorn Cichlid that sold in Malaysia in 2009 for $600,000 USD. – Size: 10-16 inches   Colour: Patterned: red, green, purple, blue, yellow – Lifespan: 10 to 12 years

Platinum Arowana - Price: $400K USD - Size: 4 Feet 9 Inch - Colour: Silver White - Lifespan: 10-15 years

Freshwater Polka Dot Stingray - Price: $100K USD - Size: 1 Feet 6 inch - Colour: Black /White /Brown - Lifespan: 5-10 years

Xingu River Ray – Price: $100k USD - Size: 11.8 to 15.7 inch - Weight: 17kg - Life Span: 14 years

Peppermint Angelfish - Cost: $30K USD - Size: 3 inch –

Colour: Orangish Red and white - Lifespan: 10-15 years

Most Expensive Fish Sold as Food

Bluefin tuna is the world's most expensive 'food' fish. In 2019, a 612-pound bluefin tuna sold in Japan for $3.1 million, breaking the record for the most expensive fish ever sold. Bluefin tuna, which is used to make sushi, has become more expensive as the species has become endangered.

Lifespans of Fish

Longest Lifespans

The Greenland shark (Somniosus microcephalus) can live for up to 392 years, making it not only the longest-living animal, but also the longest-living vertebrate.

Radiocarbon dating of eye lens nuclei from 28 female Greenland sharks (81-502 cm total length) revealed a minimum lifespan of 272 years in a 2015 study. Only the smallest sharks (220 cm) showed signs of the radiocarbon bomb pulse, which was a marker of the early 1960s.

This deep-sea fish grows at a rate of about 1 centimetre (0.4 inch) per year and does not reach sexual maturity until it is 150 years old. It is widely distributed in the cold waters of the North Atlantic, which is thought to contribute to its long life.

Other Long-Living Fish

Other long-living fish include the Rougheye Rockfish, which can survive for more than 205 years.

Some species of sturgeon are known to survive for up to 200 years.

Orange Roughy has a maximum lifespan of 150 years.

Black Seabream - have a maximum lifespan of 100 years.

The Bowhead Sculpin has a maximum lifespan of 95 years.

Pacific Halibut - has a maximum lifespan of 55 years.

Shortest Lifespans

The Sign Eviota, Eviota sigillata, a small coral reef fish that completes its entire life cycle in eight weeks (56 days), is thought to be the fish with the shortest lifespan. This species has the shortest lifespan of any vertebrate.

The Seven-figure pygmy goby (Eviota sigillata), which lives an average of 59 days, is another fish with the shortest average life span.

How Scientist Determine Age

Researchers interested in determining a fish age look for structures which increase incrementally with age. The most commonly used techniques involve counting natural growth rings on the scales and otoliths (ear bones). The rings, which are like the annual rings on tree trunks, indicate seasonal changes in fish growth.

Figure 31 Close up of fish scales showing growth rings

Species Focus
Bass in the USA

Figure 32 Largemouth Bass

There are several species of bass found in the United States.

Some of these species are restricted to specific regions of the country, while others are found throughout the country.

Largemouth bass and smallmouth bass are among the most popular game fish in the US and are found in many bodies of water across the country.

Bass Fishing Contests

There are many bass fishing contests in the USA, some of which offer large cash prizes. One of the biggest organizations for bass fishing tournaments is B.A.S.S. (Bass Anglers Sportsman Society) which hosts several events, including the Bassmaster Classic, Elite Series, Bassmaster Opens, and Toyota Bassmaster Angler of the Year.

The largest cash payout of any single freshwater fishing tournament in history is believed to be a $1 million cash prize, won by the National Championship team at the Bass Pro Shops US Open National Bass Fishing Amateur Team Championships

Bass Species

Here are the maximum reported sizes for some of the most common bass species found in the United States:

Largemouth bass: The largest recorded largemouth bass was caught in Georgia and weighed 22 pounds 4 ounces. Largemouth bass typically grow up to 22-24 inches in length and weigh up to 10-12 pounds.

Smallmouth bass: The largest recorded smallmouth bass was caught in Tennessee and weighed 11 pounds 15 ounces. Smallmouth bass generally grow up to 16-20 inches in length and weigh up to 4-5 pounds.

Spotted bass: The largest recorded spotted bass was caught in Alabama and weighed 9 pounds 8 ounces. Spotted bass typically grow up to 15-20 inches in length and weigh up to 3-4 pounds.

Guadalupe bass: The largest recorded Guadalupe bass was caught in Texas and weighed 3 pounds 11 ounces. Guadalupe bass usually grow up to 10-14 inches in length and weigh up to 1-2 pounds.

Redeye bass: The largest recorded redeye bass was caught in Georgia and weighed 3 pounds 1 ounce. Redeye bass usually grow up to 10-12 inches in length and weigh up to 1 pound.

Shoal bass: The largest recorded shoal bass was caught in

Georgia and weighed 8 pounds 12 ounces. Shoal bass typically grow up to 20-22 inches in length and weigh up to 4-5 pounds.

World Record Bass

The current world record is an impressive 22.31lb bass that was caught by Manabu Kurita at Lake Biwa in Japan, in 2009.

Second spot goes to George Perry, who caught a 22.25lb largemouth bass at Lake Montgomery in Georgia in 1932.

Catfish

Figure 33 Catfish

Catfish have been around for many millions of years. According to fossil evidence, catfish have been swimming in the world's oceans and freshwater bodies for over 50 million years. Some of the earliest discovered catfish fossils date back to the Eocene period.

There are over 3,000 catfish species in the world. Some examples include flathead catfish, Wels catfish, Goonch catfish,

Paraiba catfish, and Mekong catfish.

The walking catfish is an unusual species that "walks" on land between bodies of water using its pectoral fins.

Catfish have taste receptors all over their bodies, including their fins and tails, which aids them in finding food in murky waters.

Depending on the species, catfish may have up to four pairs of barbels, including nasal, maxillary (on each side of the mouth), and two pairs of chin barbels. Barbels on catfish always occur in pairs.

Due to the importance of barbels and chemoreception in detecting food, catfish typically have small eyes.

Some catfish species can generate an electrical current for communication and self-defence.

Noodling is a type of fishing that uses only the hands and feet to catch fish. It is common in the southern United States. Here are some of the largest fish ever caught with a fishing lure: In 1975, Lee McFarlin caught a 121-pound flathead catfish in Oklahoma. In 2001, Jackie Bibby caught a 103-pound flathead catfish in Texas.

A Mekong giant catfish caught in Thailand's Mae Klong River in May 2005 is thought to be the largest catfish ever caught with a rod and reel. The fish weighed 646 pounds and measured 9 feet long.

Trout

Figure 34 Rainbow Trout

Trout Species

There are around 50 species of trout found throughout the world. Some of the most well-known species include:

- Rainbow Trout (Oncorhynchus mykiss)

- Brown Trout (Salmo trutta)

- Brook Trout (Salvelinus fontinalis)

- Lake Trout (Salvelinus namaycush)

- Cutthroat Trout (Oncorhynchus clarkii)

- Golden Trout (Oncorhynchus aguabonita)

- Steelhead Trout (Oncorhynchus mykiss)

Rod-Caught World Records

The International Game Fish Association All-Tackle World Record for Lake trout stands at 32.65 kg (72 lb 0 oz), caught in Great Bear Lake, Northwest Territories, Canada in 19-Aug-1995. A 73lb lake trout caught in an undisclosed Colorado lake in 2023, may be the largest caught of this species on a line and could become the new world record.

North American Records

Rainbow Trout (Oncorhynchus mykiss) 48 lb 0oz Diefenbaker Reservoir Canada 2009

Cutthroat trout (Oncorhynchus clarkia) 41lb 0oz Pyramid Lake USA 1925

Biggest Trout Rod-Caught UK

Brown Trout Salmo trutta 31lb 12oz Loch Awe 2002

Salmon

Figure 35 Salmon

There are several species of salmon, including:

Atlantic salmon (Salmo salar)

Chinook salmon (Oncorhynchus tshawytscha)

Coho salmon (Oncorhynchus kisutch)

Pink salmon (Oncorhynchus gorbuscha)

Sockeye salmon (Oncorhynchus nerka)

Chum salmon (Oncorhynchus keta)

Note that some sources classify the Pacific salmon species (Chinook, Coho, Pink, Sockeye, and Chum) under the genus Oncorhynchus, while others use the genus Salmo for Atlantic salmon only.

Coho salmon (Oncorhynchus kisutch) - found in the North Pacific Ocean and commonly caught in Alaska and British Columbia.

Sockeye salmon (Oncorhynchus nerka) - found in the North Pacific Ocean and commonly caught in Alaska and British Columbia.

Chum salmon (Oncorhynchus keta) - found in the northern Pacific Ocean and commonly caught in Alaska and British Columbia.

Several additional species of salmon found in the world, including:

Cherry salmon (Oncorhynchus masou) - native to the western Pacific Ocean, particularly in Japan and Korea.

Pink salmon (Oncorhynchus gorbuscha) - found in the northern Pacific Ocean and commonly caught in Alaska and British Columbia.

Masu salmon (Oncorhynchus masou) - found in the western Pacific Ocean, particularly in Japan and Russia.

Atlantic salmon (Salmo salar) - found in the North Atlantic Ocean and commonly caught in Scotland, Norway, Canada, and the north-eastern United States.

UK Rod-Caught Record

The biggest recorded Atlantic salmon caught in the UK was caught on the River Tay in Scotland in 1922. The fish weighed 64 pounds and was caught by Miss Georgina Ballantine.

Figure 36 Miss G. Ballantine with 64lb Salmon 1922

USA Rod-Caught Record

The biggest salmon ever caught on rod and line in the USA weighed 97.25 pounds and was caught in the Kenai River in Alaska in 1985. The fish was a Chinook salmon.

Pike Folklore

Figure 37 Pike

Here are some examples of legends about gigantic pike:

A Scottish legend tells of a colossal pike that once lived in Loch Arkaig, a freshwater loch in the Scottish Highlands. The pike was said to be so large that it could consume a young deer whole.

The Great Northern Pike of Lake Windermere: According to this English legend, a massive pike once lived in Lake Windermere in the Lake District. The pike was reportedly over 30 feet long and devoured several swimmers and boaters.

An American legend describes a monstrous pike that once resided in Tennessee's Bledsoe Creek. It was reported that the pike measured over 10 feet in length and had a mouth large enough to consume a child.

The Old Man of the Lake is a legend about a gigantic pike that resides in Oregon's Crater Lake. It is said that the pike is over 30 feet long and has lived in the lake for centuries.

The Laxen of Jostedalsvatnet is a Norwegian legend about a giant pike that resided in Norway's largest lake, Jostedalsvatnet. It was said that the pike was so large that it could consume a man whole.

World Record Rod-Caught Pike
Two pike captured in the same German lake share the current International Game Fish Association (IGFA) all-tackle world record for pike. The first was captured by Lothar Louis in 1986 and weighed 55 pounds and one ounce; the second was caught by Arno Wilhelm in 1992 and weighed 55 pounds and seven ounces.

Other Huge Pike Captures
A 58-inch-long pike caught in Lough Derg, Ireland, in 1929, weighed an estimated 59 pounds, but was not officially recorded.

A 58-inch pike caught in the Baltic Sea, near Gävle, Sweden, in 2014, weighed 55 pounds and 13 ounces, but was not officially recorded as well.

A 54-inch-long pike caught in Lake Winnipeg, Canada, in 1968, weighed 53 pounds and 2 ounces.

A 52-inch-long pike caught in Lake of Grefeern, Germany, in 1984, weighed 51 pounds.

Carp Folklore

Figure 38 Common Carp

Carp Myths and Tales

For centuries, giant carp have been revered in mythology and folklore around the world, and there are numerous stories and legends about them. Here are a few examples:

According to the Chinese legend of the "Koi Gate," a gigantic carp swam up a waterfall to the "Dragon's Gate" at the summit, where it was transformed into a dragon. This tale has come to represent tenacity, ambition, and success.

Carp are also associated with luck and success in Japan, and "Koi Nobori," or "Carp Streamers," are a popular Children's Day festival decoration. The streamers, the largest of which represents the father, are hung to represent the family's wish for their children to be as strong and successful as carp.

Carp are revered as sacred in certain parts of India and are frequently released into lakes and ponds during religious festivals. There are also stories of giant carp inhabiting the holy Ganges River, with some claiming that the largest can grow to be over 6 metres long.

Izzak Walton – The Compleat Angler

In 1653 Izaak Walton wrote in The Compleat Angler, "The Carp is the queen of rivers; a stately, a good, and a very subtle fish; that was not at first bred, nor hath been long in England, but is now naturalised."

Redmire Pool

Redmire Pool is close to Ross-on-Wye in the English county of Herefordshire. Expert anglers think of it as the home of carp fishing in the UK, even though it is only 3 acres (1.2 ha) in size.

On September 13, 1952, Richard Walker caught a carp that weighed 44 pounds (20 kg) and set a British record. This made the water famous. The fish, which was a common carp, was moved to the aquarium at the London Zoo. Walker gave her the name Ravioli at first, but the staff at the London Zoo changed it to Clarissa.

Giant Carp Captures worldwide

There are many accounts of gigantic carp in the Danube River in Europe, including the legend of the 100-pound "Giant Carp of Karnten" in Austria.

In May of 2011, "The Siamese Giant Carp," weighing 232 pounds, was captured in a private lake in Thailand.

Sharks

Figure 39 Great White shark

Prehistoric Sharks

Scientists believe sharks first appeared in the ocean around 455 million years ago, based on fossilised scales discovered in Australia and the United States.

The oldest known species of living shark in the Goblin Shark that has been around for 120 million years. The second oldest is the Frilled Shark that has been around for 80 million years.

Megalodon - This prehistoric shark lived approximately 23 to 3.6 million years ago and is believed to have reached a maximum length of 60 feet. Despite being extinct, the Megalodon is the subject of many myths and legends.

Distribution

There are around 500 known species of sharks, and they live

in every ocean on the planet.

Physiology

Sharks do not have bones. They are a special type of fish known as "elasmobranchs", - fish made of cartilaginous tissues. Their cartilaginous skeletons are much lighter than true bone.

Sharks do not have swim bladders. The oil in their large livers gives them buoyancy and keeps them from sinking to the bottom of the ocean.

Many shark species must always be in motion to direct the flow of water over the gills which absorb oxygen for respiration.

Placoid scales, also known as dermal denticles, are tiny tooth-like structures that give the skin of sharks a sandpaper-like texture. These scales point toward the shark's tail and aid in reducing friction when it swims. Before sandpaper was invented, people used shark skin, called shagreen, to smooth and polish wood.

Swimming Speeds

The average shark can cruise at about 5 miles per hour. Some sharks, such as the shortfin mako and the great white, can reach speeds of up to 60 miles per hour, while others, such as the tiger and the blue shark, can reach speeds of up to 40 and 25 miles per hour, respectively.

Size Range

The world's smallest sharks include: The spined pygmy shark is only 7 inches long, dwarf lantern that is only grows to 6 inches. Recently, scientists discovered a new species of shark measuring only 5 1/2 inches in length: the American Pocket Shark.

Whale sharks are the biggest fish in the ocean. They can grow to over 40 feet and weigh as much as 40 tons. Basking sharks are the world's second largest fish, growing as long as 32 feet and weighing more than five tons.

Shark Attacks

The first written account of a shark attack is found in Herodotus' (c. 484–425 B.C.) description of hordes of "monsters" devouring the shipwrecked sailors of the Persian fleet.

The Florida Museum of Natural History's International Shark Attack File investigated shark-human interactions worldwide in 2022. The total of 57 confirmed unprovoked cases around the world in 2022 is less than the average of 70 each year over the last five years (2017-2021). There were nine shark-related fatalities that year, five of which are assigned as unprovoked. This number is the same as the global average of six unprovoked deaths per year over the past five years.

Sharks under Threat

An estimated 100 million sharks are killed annually across the globe, a staggeringly high number that exceeds the rate of recovery for these populations.

Scientists point to one main contributing factor that is causing this rapid decline in total world shark population is shark finning. A barbaric practise, where fins are cut from sharks, which are then thrown back into the water to die. The practice has increased over the past decade due to the increasing demand for fins (for shark fin soup).

The rate of finning has increased dramatically since 1970, which accounts for the drastic decrease in shark population since then.

Many sharks are under threat, listed by International Union for the Conservation of Nature (IUCN) from vulnerable to critically endangered.

Figure 40 Endangered species

Extinct & Endangered Fish Species

Critically Endangered Species Definition

Status definition: A species that is as facing an extremely high risk of extinction.

Critically Endangered Fish Species

The International Union for Conservation of Nature (IUCN) listed 1,000 critically endangered fish species, including 87 which are tagged as possibly extinct.

These include:

The Ganges shark (Glyphis gangeticus) requiem shark found in the Ganges River (Padma River) and the Brahmaputra River of India and Bangladesh.

The Maltese skate (Leucoraja melitensis), or Maltese ray, is a species of fish in the family Rajidae. It is a rare endemic species from the Mediterranean Sea, found in the coastal waters of Algeria, Italy, Malta, Tunisia, Greece, and Turkey.

The Chinese sturgeon (Acipenser sinensis), Historically, this anadromous fish was found in China, Japan, and the Korean Peninsula, but it has been extirpated from most regions due to habitat loss and overfishing. It is strictly protected by the Chinese government, named a "national treasure".

The Blind cave loach (Nemacheilus troglocataractus) is a species of troglobitic stone loach endemic to Thailand. It is only known from one subterranean stream in the Sai Yok Noi cave. The blind cave loach has no eyes and lacks pigmentation.

The European eel is a critically endangered species. Since the 1970s, the numbers of eels reaching Europe is thought to have declined by around 90%. Contributing factors include overfishing, parasites, barriers to migration such as hydroelectric dams, and natural changes in the North Atlantic oscillation, Gulf Stream.

Figure 41 European Eel

Endangered Species Definition
Status definition: A species that is seriously at risk of extinction.

Endangered Fish Species

In September 2016, the International Union for Conservation of Nature (IUCN) listed 643 endangered fish species.

These include:

The Schelly (Coregonus stigmaticus) is a living freshwater fish of the salmon family, endemic to four lakes in the Lake District, England. It is found in Brothers Water, Haweswater, Red Tarn, and Ullswater, and its population appears to be stable in all but Haweswater, where it appears to be declining.

The Death Valley pupfish (Cyprinodon salinus), also known as Salt Creek pupfish, is a small species of fish in the family Cyprinodontidae found only in Death Valley National Park, California, United States.

The Dead Sea toothcarp (Aphanius dispar richardsoni) is a subspecies of the Arabian toothcarp that is endemic to the Dead Sea basin. It is threatened by water fluctuation, and the introduction of non-native fish species.

Recently Extinct Species Definition
Status definition: Extinction is the termination of a species by the death of its last member. A species may become functionally extinct before the death of its last member if it loses the ability to reproduce and recover.

Recently Extinct Fish Species

As of September 2016, the International Union for Conservation of Nature (IUCN) lists 65 extinct fish species, 87 possibly extinct fish species, and six extinct in the wild fish species.

The Lost shark (Carcharhinus obsoletus), previously known as the false smalltail shark, is a possibly extinct species of requiem shark (family Carcharhinidae). Only three specimens of this species are known, found in Borneo, Vietnam, and Thailand. For more than 80 years, no individuals have been found.

The Mediterranean sand tiger shark (Carcharias taurus europaeus) was a population of sand tiger shark that inhabited the Mediterranean Sea. In 2001, its population was estimated to be less than 200. The most recent confirmed record was a specimen caught in the Mediterranean Sea in 2003. After not being seen in nearly two decades, the species is thought to be extinct.

The Chinese paddlefish (Psephurus gladius), also known as the Chinese swordfish, is an extinct fish species native to China's Yangtze and Yellow River basins. It was one of the largest freshwater fish species, with specimens reaching three metres (ten feet) and possibly seven metres (twenty-three feet). The Chinese paddlefish was officially declared extinct in 2022, with extinction determined to be 2005 and no later than 2010. The primary cause of its extinction was the construction of the Gezhouba and Three Gorges dams, which caused population fragmentation and obstructed spawning migration.

The New Zealand grayling (Prototroctes oxyrhynchus) is an extinct fish species native to New Zealand. It was known to the Māori by many names, including pokororo, paneroro, kanae-kura, and most commonly, upokororo. The last sighting of the New Zealand grayling was in 1923, and it was declared extinct in 2018. The cause of the New Zealand grayling's extinction is unknown.

Most Peculiar Fish Names

Barreleye (Macropinna microstoma)

Blobfish (Psychrolutes marcidus)

Coffinfish (Chaunax endeavouri)

Devil Ray (Mobula mobular)

Fangblenny (Meiacanthus grammistes)

Four-Eyed Fish (Anableps Anableps)

Goblin Shark (Mitsukurina owstoni)

Gulper Eel (Eurypharynx pelecanoides)

Hairy Angler (Antennarius striatus)

Lanternfish (Myctophidae family)

Leaf Scorpionfish (Taenianotus triacanthus)

Longnose Batfish (Ogcocephalus corniger)

Lumpsucker Cyclopterus lumpus

Naked Mole Ratfish (Chimaera monstrosa)

Pacific Spiny Lumpsucker (Eumicrotremus orbis)

Racoon Butterflyfish (Chaetodon lunula)

Sarcastic Fringehead (Neoclinus blanchardi)

Stargazer (Uranoscopidae family)

Dangerous Fish

The Stonefish is one of the world's most poisonous fish. Its venom can cause severe pain, paralysis, and even death. Swimmers often step on the fish by mistake because it is well camouflaged.

Figure 42 Stonefish

Pufferfish contain tetrodotoxin, a neurotoxin that can induce paralysis, respiratory failure, and death. Regardless, certain pufferfish species are considered delicacies in some cultures, but they must be carefully prepared to remove the poisonous parts.

Electric eels, despite their name, are a type of knifefish, not true eels. They can generate 600-volt electric shocks, which they use for foraging and self-defence. The discharge of an electric eel can be fatal to humans.

The Candiru is a parasitic catfish found in the Amazon Basin. It is notorious for swimming into human urethras, where it can cause crippling pain and potentially fatal complications.

The venomous, Indo-Pacific-native lionfish has become an invasive species in the Caribbean and Gulf of Mexico. Its venomous spines can cause severe pain, nausea, and even paralysis.

The goliath tigerfish is a large predatory fish found in African rivers. It has razor-sharp fangs up to 6 inches long and has been known to attack humans who invade its territory.

The tail barb of the Stingray, a type of cartilaginous fish, is pointed and poisonous. Even though they are not aggressive, accidental encounters can result in agonising and potentially fatal injuries. Steve Irwin, an Australian zookeeper, conservationist, and television personality, was killed by a stingray while filming in the Great Barrier Reef on September 4, 2006. The barb of the stingray pierced his chest, causing severe trauma.

Figure 43 Stingray

Photo and illustration credits

Photos and illustrations (including cover photos): Depositphotos

Additional images:

Page 26 Shark. Marcelo Cidrack. Unsplash.

Page 35 Lateral line illustration. Thomas.Haslwanter, CC BY-SA 3.0 https://creativecommons.org/licenses/by-sa/3.0, via Wikimedia Commons

Page 43 Julimes pupfish (Cyprinodon julimes). Mexicankillis/Mauricio De la Maza-Benignos, CC BY-SA 3.0 https://creativecommons.org/licenses/by-sa/3.0, via Wikimedia Commons

Page 55 Clownfish. Sebastian Pena Lambarri on Unsplash

Page 60 Pseudoliparis swirei. Gerringer M. E., Linley T. D., Jamieson A. J., Goetze E., Drazen J. C., CC BY 3.0 https://creativecommons.org/licenses/by/3.0, via Wikimedia Commons

Page 61 Blobfish. Photographer: James Joel https://www.flickr.com/photos/98701585@N02/9351589556